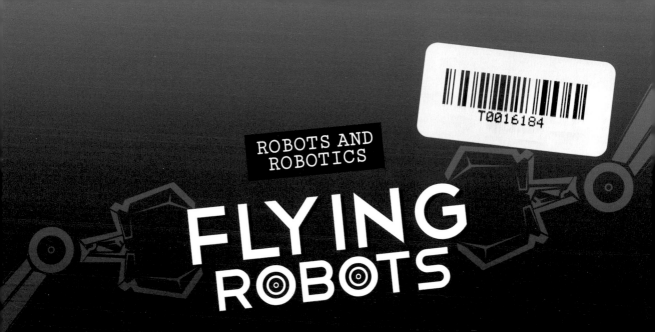

ROBOTS AND ROBOTICS

FLYING ROBOTS

DANIEL R. FAUST

PowerKiDS
press

New York

Published in 2017 by The Rosen Publishing Group, Inc.
29 East 21st Street, New York, NY 10010

First Edition

Editor: Caitie McAneney
Book Design: Reann Nye

Photo Credits: Cover funkyfrogstock/Shutterstock.com; p. 4 Supannee Hickman/Shutterstock.com; p. 5 B.Stefanov/Shutterstock.com; p. 6 produktionsbuero TINUS/Shutterstock.com; p. 7 Andrei Kholmov/Shutterstock.com; p. 8 seregalsv/Shutterstock.com; pp. 9 (main image, battery, propellers), 17 marekuliasz/Shutterstock.com; p. 10 Kletr/Shutterstock.com; p. 12 dade72/Shutterstock.com; p. 13 https://commons.wikimedia.org/wiki/File:Flytech_Dragonfly.jpg; p. 15 Mike Focus/Shutterstock.com; p. 16 Tyler Olson/Shutterstock.com; p. 18 Frank Mullen/WireImage/Getty Images; p. 19 Umkehrer/Shutterstock.com; p. 20 BERTRAND LANGLOIS/AFP/Getty Images; p. 21 David Ramos/Getty Images News/Getty Images; p. 23 MICHAEL B. THOMAS/AFP/Getty Images; p. 24 Ulrich Baumgarten/Getty Images; p. 25 Juan Silva/Moment Mobile/Getty Images; p. 26 Bloomberg/Getty Images; p. 27 p_ponomareva/Shutterstock.com; p. 29 goodluz/Shutterstock.com; p. 30 SKatzenberger/Shutterstock.com.

Library of Congress Cataloging-in-Publication Data

Names: Faust, Daniel R., author.
Title: Flying robots / Daniel R. Faust.
Description: New York : PowerKids Press, [2017] | Series: Robots and robotics
  | Includes index.
Identifiers: LCCN 2016006794 | ISBN 9781499421675 (pbk.) | ISBN 9781499421699 (library bound) | ISBN 9781499421682 (6 pack)
Subjects: LCSH: Robotics–Juvenile literature. | Drone aircraft–Juvenile
  literature. | Micro air vehicles–Juvenile literature.
Classification: LCC TJ211.2 .F39 2017 | DDC 629.8/92–dc23
LC record available at http://lccn.loc.gov/2016006794

Manufactured in the United States of America

CPSIA Compliance Information: Batch #BS16PK: For Further Information contact Rosen Publishing, New York, New York at 1-800-237-9932

CONTENTS

ROBOTS READY FOR TAKEOFF!

Have you ever seen a robot flying through the sky? When most of us think about robots, we picture robots from movies, TV shows, and books. These robots are often giant machines that look like people. These kinds of robots are still works of fiction, but there are real robots in the world. You might just have to look up to the sky to find them.

Although they make for exciting entertainment, the humanlike robots from your favorite TV shows and movies are nothing like real robots.

The earliest modern robots were large machines built to work in factories. They had limited **mobility** and could only perform simple tasks, such as painting or welding. Over time, people developed robots that are smaller and more **complex**. Some are even light enough to take to the air. You may know these flying robots as drones, or unmanned aerial vehicles (UAV).

WHAT'S A ROBOT?

A robot is a mechanical device that's built to perform a task or a series of tasks. People can program robots to work on their own or they can control a robot in person. Robots can perform their tasks the same way, over and over, for hours at a time.

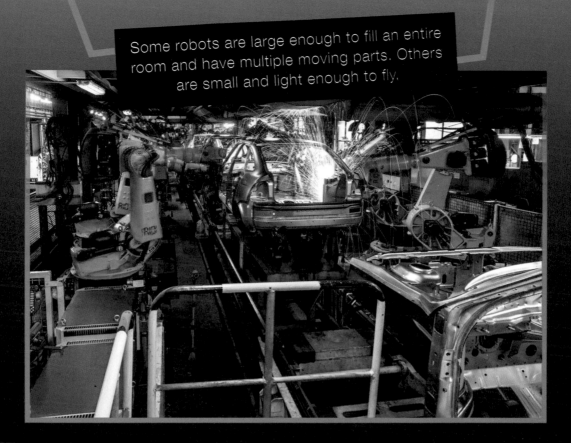

Some robots are large enough to fill an entire room and have multiple moving parts. Others are small and light enough to fly.

People used the first modern robots to replace workers on assembly lines in factories because they could perform the same task repeatedly. Today, factories still use robots to make products such as computers and cars. Robots can also be used to save lives during emergencies. A robot can be used in the place of a human for **dangerous** jobs, such as flying over wildfires and entering enemy territory during war. Today, robots are used in almost every aspect of human life, from work to play.

Robots come in a surprising number of shapes and sizes, and they can perform any number of tasks. But whatever a robot might look like or whatever job it may do, most share the same basic components, or parts. Basic parts of a robot include the sensors, frame, motors, effectors, and controller. Even though flying robots are in a class of their own, they need basic robot parts to work, too.

Sensors are the parts of the robot that gather information about the robot's surroundings, which helps guide its movement and behavior. The simplest robots have sensors that prevent them from hitting **obstacles**, such as walls, furniture, other robots, or people. Some robots have cameras and microphones that act like eyes and ears.

RADIO TRANSMITTER
allows owner to control the
hexacopter's movements

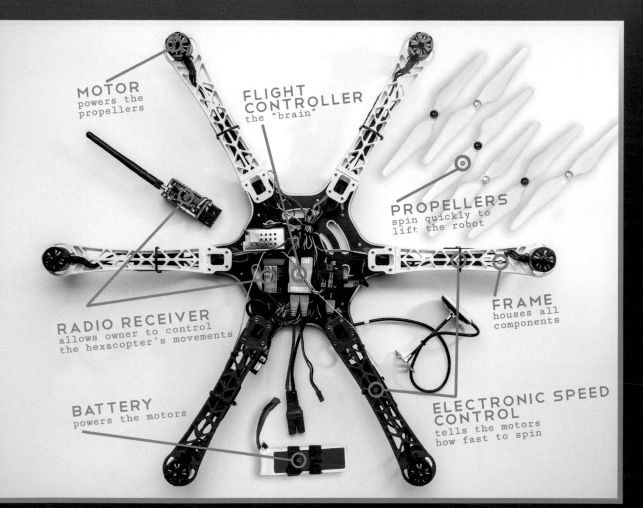

MOTOR
powers the
propellers

**FLIGHT
CONTROLLER**
the "brain"

PROPELLERS
spin quickly to
lift the robot

RADIO RECEIVER
allows owner to control
the hexacopter's movements

FRAME
houses all
components

BATTERY
powers the motors

**ELECTRONIC SPEED
CONTROL**
tells the motors
how fast to spin

Some robots are equipped with specialized sensors that allow them to detect temperature, air pressure, and changes to the Earth's magnetic field. These flying robots are ready for extreme missions.

The frame of a robot keeps all the important parts together and gives it a specific shape. It can be made from wood, plastic, or metal. Effectors help the robot **interact** directly with its **environment**. These parts allow a robot to perform specific tasks. Claws, hammers, shovels, and screwdrivers are examples of effectors.

Motors, called actuators, drive the action of the robot. For flying robots, you need a motor for each propeller, or spinning blade. Quadcopters have four propellers, so they need four motors.

The final basic component of a flying robot is the flight controller. The flight controller is a computer that acts like the robot's brain. It processes information about the robot's surroundings using information gathered through the sensors. Then, it moves the robot according to a series of preprogrammed actions.

THE ENGINEERING DESIGN PROCESS

STEP ONE: ASK

What do you want your robot to do? How have other people made similar robots?

STEP TWO: IMAGINE

Brainstorm ideas. Pick the best idea.

STEP THREE: PLAN

Draw a diagram. Gather materials.

STEP FOUR: CREATE

Follow the plan. Test the results.

STEP FIVE: IMPROVE

How can I make my design better? Repeat the steps.

Now that you know the basic parts of a robot, you can start to design your own.

Many flying robots, or drones, resemble airplanes and helicopters. The men and women who designed the first drones applied the basic scientific principles of lift, thrust, drag, and weight that keep aircraft in the air. Today, many robotics engineers are inspired by flight in the natural world.

THE FOUR FORCES OF FLIGHT

To understand how aircraft fly, you need to know about the four basic principles of flight. Lift is the upward force acting on an object. Thrust is the force that moves an object in a given direction—forward, backward, left, or right. Drag is the force that acts upon a body in the opposite direction of the body's movement. Weight is the force of gravity acting upon a body. Engineers have to ask how heavy the aircraft is to determine how much power is needed to lift it into the air.

Flapping-wing robots are designed to copy the motion of insect wings. Robots based on this design tend to be faster and more maneuverable than robots built to resemble planes and helicopters.

FLYTECH DRAGONFLY

Modern flying robots are fast and **maneuverable**, but they're still slow and clumsy when compared to a bee or a dragonfly. Scientists and engineers have studied insect bodies for years in an attempt to develop tiny, insect-like robots called microdrones. Today, engineers are building tiny robots with flexible bodies and flapping wings. Unlike other flying robots, these microdrones can fit in tiny spaces, zip around corners, and better avoid crashing into obstacles.

SPECIAL DELIVERY

Can you imagine ordering groceries online and having a drone drop them at your house? Drones might be a method of delivery in the future! In 2015, the **Federal Aviation Administration** (FAA) decided to allow the online store Amazon to research, test, and train the drones that might one day be part of its delivery system. The plan calls for Amazon's drones to deliver some packages less than 5 pounds (2.7 kg) within 30 minutes.

Google started working on a similar delivery system known as Project Wing. Delivery drones could allow businesses to ship products without a delivery person. This means businesses can reach more customers. This kind of delivery could totally change the way people shop for and receive their products.

Some companies are pursuing technology to use flying robots to deliver small packages quickly and cheaply.

THIS SIDE UP

LIGHTS! CAMERA! ROBOTS!

Taking pictures from above is called aerial photography. During World Wars I and II, aerial photography was used for reconnaissance, or finding information about an enemy. The first commercial aerial photography company was formed in 1919. Early aerial photography was used for surveying and map-making purposes. Soon, the growing motion picture industry started to use aerial video cameras.

CAMERA DRONE

A number of production companies have replaced helicopter-mounted cameras with camera drones. These small flying robots can be used to film difficult shots and angles.

Helicopters equipped with video cameras are a common sight on the sets of many motion pictures, television shows, and commercials. The overhead footage captured by helicopter-mounted cameras gives an audience a larger view from above. However, helicopters are expensive. Flying drones equipped with cameras are cheaper and often safer than helicopters. Plus, they can get up close to the action.

THEME PARK ROBOTS

From laser shows to **animatronic** creatures, amusement and theme parks use the latest technologies to entertain their visitors. Theme parks hire engineers to create awesome rides and attractions. In the future, theme parks may use flying robots as the centerpieces of their attractions.

ANIMATRONIC T.REX

Fireworks are a common sight over many amusement parks. One day, fleets of tiny, bright flying robots may replace these brilliant displays.

Some theme parks might someday use flying robots to perform dazzling light shows every night. Parks might also use flying robots as puppeteers in the sky. The robots could work together to operate giant puppets. Flying robots could also carry giant screens onto which movies and images could be projected. Other robots could be used as flying **pixels**. Hundreds of these tiny flying robots could come together to paint huge, moving pictures in the sky.

SEARCH AND RESCUE

When someone is lost in the wilderness, every second counts. Searching by foot can take hours or even days. Using drones can make it much easier to locate people who are lost. Equipped with cameras, these flying robots can search an area of land in a fraction of the time it could take a human search party. Some of these robots are even equipped with special night-vision cameras, which make it easier to find people in the dark.

MANHUNT!

There are organizations whose members offer to use drones to help find people who are lost. Some even specialize in finding lost pets. However, law enforcement agencies also use flying robots to locate suspects and track escaped prisoners. Although some agencies use equipment borrowed from the military, many of the drones used by the police and other agencies are not very different from the kind you can buy online or at a hobby store.

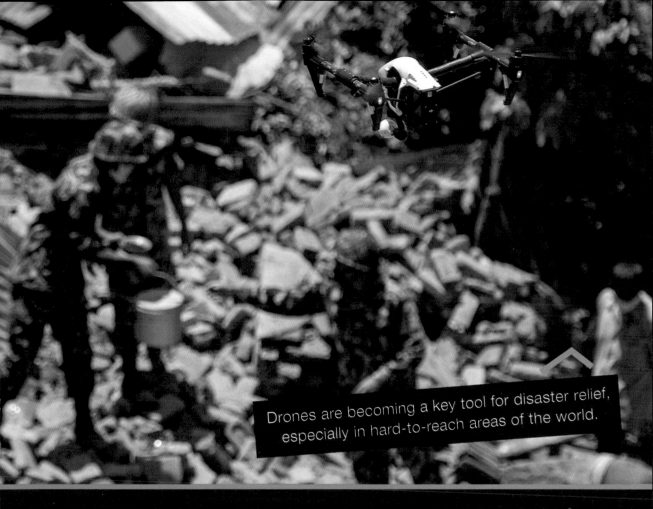

Drones are becoming a key tool for disaster relief, especially in hard-to-reach areas of the world.

Flying robots can also help find people after a natural disaster, such as an earthquake or hurricane. These robots can be sent into an area immediately after the disaster instead of waiting for it to be safe for human rescuers. The tiny machines can check for survivors in even the smallest spaces. Some drones are used to deliver food and medical supplies to people who are trapped in hard-to-reach places.

Like Hollywood studios, members of the **news media** often require aerial footage to accompany their reports. They often use helicopters to capture this aerial footage. Helicopters are also used for traffic reports. Drones can provide a cheaper and safer alternative to news helicopters. These flying robots can also get closer to scenes and provide more detailed images and videos for the news. They can even be used to provide detailed video of traffic accidents and high-speed car chases.

News companies aren't the only ones using camera-equipped drones. In some situations, people have used drones to record footage at the scene of accidents before reporters even arrive. In recent years, drones have been used to provide eye-in-the-sky coverage of large-scale protests and events.

Sometimes, people with drones cover large events and protests to provide a different view from those offered by the news media.

SAFETY FIRST

In June 2014, the FAA approved the use of commercial drones over land for the first time. One of the world's largest energy companies, BP, was given permission to use drones to survey the equipment and pipelines at its oil field in Alaska. Flying robots have also been used to inspect buildings and other structures.

Historically, robots have been used in situations that may be too dangerous for human workers. Today, companies can keep even more workers safe by using drones.

Construction companies can use flying robots to improve safety and efficiency at jobsites. Flying robots can inspect dangerous or hard-to-reach sections of a building. They can also monitor crew progress and provide security for the construction site. Environmental scientists use drones to study climate changes, track endangered wildlife, and stop **poachers**. Drones can also be used to inspect power lines, roads, bridges, and railroad tracks.

Flying robots are important tools, but they can also be a lot of fun. Recreational drones, or drones for personal entertainment, can be found online or at your local hobby store. Some recreational drones are small enough to fit in your pocket, while others are large enough to carry cameras. Many communities have drone-flying clubs in which drone operators can meet and show off their skills.

A CAR THAT FLIES!

Self-driving cars are already in development, but what about self-flying cars? The Ehang 184 could be the first self-flying drone car. It was developed by a Chinese company and presented at the 2016 Consumer Electronics Show. The Ehang 184 weighs about 440 pounds (199.6 kg). The vehicle can be programmed to fly a single passenger a distance of about 10 miles (16 km). Do you think flying robot cars are in our future?

In addition to flying clubs, there are also clubs that specialize in drone racing. Drone operators wear special goggles that allow them to see directly through their drone's camera. Air shows are starting to introduce drone races and aerial **demonstrations**.
Camera drones are also used in the world of extreme sports to record up-close, real-time footage of snowboarders, BMX bikers, and skateboarders.

Recreational drones are usually operated by a handheld remote control. Some have **software** that allows them to be controlled by your smartphone or tablet.

HANDHELD REMOTE

BUILDING YOUR OWN

It's easy to go online and buy a drone that's ready to use right out of the box. However, if you're interested in engineering or robotics, you can also buy the separate components and build your own flying robot. You can even use a 3-D printer to produce some of the components you'll need.

If you want to use your drone to take photographs or record videos, you'll need to add a camera. You can further customize your camera drone by adding a part called a stabilizing gimbal, which helps steady the camera while the drone is in flight. Adding LED lights will allow you to fly your drone at night. You can even decorate your drone with special parts and stickers.

When you finish building your drone, weigh it. If it's more than 0.55 pounds (0.25 kg) but less than 55 pounds (25 kg), you must register it with the FAA.

THE SKIES OF TOMORROW

In the future, our world will be full of robots of all shapes, sizes, and abilities. Television and movies show a world where robots clean our homes, prepare our meals, and drive our cars. Will this fictional future become a reality? It's hard to say for sure.

However, if you look up, you might just catch a glimpse of that possible future. Flying robots exist, and every year they become more and more common. Law enforcement agencies use flying robots to help them fight crime. Filmmakers and reporters rely on drone cameras more and more. One day, it may become common to have flying robots deliver goods right to your door. With the right materials and instructions, you can even build and operate your own flying robot!

GLOSSARY

animatronic: Of, relating to, or being a puppet or similar figure that moves by means of electronic devices.

complex: Having to do with something with many parts that work together.

dangerous: Not safe.

demonstration: An event in which people gather together to watch something being done.

environment: The conditions that surround a thing and affect it.

Federal Aviation Administration: The agency of the United States government that regulates civilian air traffic over the country.

interact: To come together and have an effect on each other.

maneuverable: Able to change position easily.

mobility: The ability to move or be moved.

news media: Sources and presentation of news and information, such as TV, radio, newspapers, magazines, and Internet articles.

obstacle: Something that makes it difficult to complete an action.

pixel: Any one of the small dots that come together to form a picture on a television or computer screen.

poacher: Someone who hunts illegally.

software: Programs that run on computers and perform certain functions.

INDEX

WEBSITES

Due to the changing nature of Internet links, PowerKids Press has developed an online list of websites related to the subject of this book. This site is updated regularly. Please use this link to access the list: www.powerkidslinks.com/rar/fly